D1411918

ROCK-OLOGY
The Hard Facts
About Rocks

Famous Rocks

by Ellen Lawrence

Consultants:

Shawn W. Wallace
Department of Earth and Planetary Sciences
American Museum of Natural History, New York, New York

Kimberly Brenneman, PhD
National Institute for Early Education Research, Rutgers University
New Brunswick, New Jersey

BEARPORT
PUBLISHING

Credits

2–3, © javarman/Shutterstock; 4L, © Derek Young; 4R, © Creative Commons, Wikipedia; 5, © Frank Merfort/Shutterstock; 6–7, © Jason Patrick Ross/Shutterstock; 8R, © luxora/Shutterstock; 8–9, © Creative Commons, Wikipedia; 10–11, © Stanislav Fosenbauer/Shutterstock; 10L, © E&E Image Library/Alamy; 12R, © Christian Kober 1/Alamy; 12–13, © Arsgera/Shutterstock; 14–15, © Steve Vidler/Superstock; 15TR, © Andrew Parker/Alamy; 16, © vvoe/Shutterstock; 17, ©Yongyut Kumsri/Shutterstock; 18, © Everett Collection Inc./Alamy; 19, © Critterbiz/Shutterstock; 20, © Derek Young, © Frank Merfort/Shutterstock, © luxora/Shutterstock, © Jason Patrick Ross/Shutterstock, and © Critterbiz/Shutterstock; 21, © Steve Vidler/Superstock, © Creative Commons, Wikipedia, © Arsgera/Shutterstock, © Stanislav Fosenbauer/Shutterstock, © vvoe/Shutterstock; 22, © Ruby Tuesday Books; 23TL, © Ulla Lohmann; 23TC, © Mauricio Anton/Science Photo library; 23TR, © Doug Meek/Shutterstock; 23BL, © Dan Kaplan/Shutterstock; 23BC, © Shutterstock; 23BR, © Klev Victor/Shutterstock.

Publisher: Kenn Goin
Editorial Director: Adam Siegel
Creative Director: Spencer Brinker
Project Editor: Natalie Lunis
Photo Researcher: Ruby Tuesday Books Ltd

Library of Congress Cataloging-in-Publication Data

Lawrence, Ellen, 1967– author.
 Famous rocks / by Ellen Lawrence ; consultants: Shawn W. Wallace, Department of Earth and Planetary Sciences, American Museum of Natural History, New York, New York, Kimberly Brenneman, PhD National Institute for Early Education Research, Rutgers University, New Brunswick, New Jersey.
      pages cm.—(Rock-ology)
 Audience: Ages 5–8.
 Includes bibliographical references and index.
 ISBN 978-1-62724-297-4 (library binding)—ISBN 1-62724-297-X (library binding)
 1. Rocks—Juvenile literature. 2. Natural monuments—Juvenile literature. I. Title.
 QH75.L366 2015
 552—dc23

2014011761

10 9 8 7 6 5 4 3 2 1

Contents

A World of Amazing Rocks

Earth is a very rocky place.

There are high mountains, deep **canyons**, and towering cliffs.

Some of Earth's rocks are famous for their size.

Others are famous for their strange shapes.

a bridge made of rocks on Mount Tai in China

Turnip Rock Island, Lake Huron, Michigan

One of the most famous rocks in the United States is Half Dome in California's Yosemite National Park. Half Dome is made of a kind of rock called granite. It is shaped like a dome that has been sliced in half.

Another very famous rocky place in the United States is the Grand Canyon. How do you think the canyon formed?

5

The Grand Canyon

The Grand Canyon in Arizona is one of the most famous rocky places on Earth.

Five million years ago, however, there was no Grand Canyon.

There was only a huge area of dry, rocky land.

Then the Colorado River began to flow over the land.

Over millions of years, the rushing river water cut through the rock, carving out the canyon.

The Grand Canyon is 277 miles (446 km) long. At its widest point, it is 18 miles (29 km) wide. In some places, it is more than 1 mile (1.6 km) deep.

Grand Canyon

Colorado River

Making the Grand Canyon

river

❶ A river cuts into rock, making a channel, or pathway.

river

❷ As the river flows, the channel grows deeper and deeper and becomes a canyon.

river

❸ Rainwater and melted snow wash down the sides of the canyon, breaking away pieces of rock. As the sides of the canyon wear away, it becomes wider and wider.

Rocky Hoodoos

At Bryce Canyon in Utah, snow and rain have created strange rocky shapes called hoodoos.

How?

Sometimes melted snow trickles into a crack in a large chunk of rock.

When the weather gets colder, the water freezes.

As the water becomes ice, it expands, or gets bigger, pushing the crack in the rock open.

Finally, the rock splits and pieces break off, creating a new rocky shape.

a hoodoo up close

Rain also helps to create the tall, thin shapes of the hoodoos at Bryce Canyon. As rain washes over the rocks, it breaks off tiny pieces.

hoodoos

A Giant Rock Called Uluru

Rising up from a desert in Australia is a giant rock called Uluru (oo-luh-ROO).

It is so big that it takes a person nearly two hours to walk around it.

Aborigine people of Australia have lived near Uluru for thousands of years.

Their **ancestors** painted pictures and symbols inside caves in the rock.

Today, Aborigine people still sometimes make rock paintings on Uluru.

Aborigine rock painting

Uluru

Uluru is the ancient Aborigine name for the rock. It is also known as Ayers Rock. It was given this name in 1873 by an explorer named William Gosse. He named it after Australia's leader, Sir Henry Ayers.

The World's Tallest Mountain

Asia's Mount Everest is the tallest mountain on Earth.

It is 5.5 miles (8.8 km) high.

It takes climbers about 40 days to make the dangerous climb to the mountain's top.

There, the wind blows with the same power as a hurricane.

It is so cold that temperatures can be as low as -100°F (-73°C).

mountain climbers on Mount Everest

Mount Everest

Mount Everest is made of many different kinds of rock, including limestone, marble, and granite. Most of the mountain's rock is covered by snow and ice, however.

An Ancient Stone Circle

Many famous rocks, such as Mount Everest, were created by nature.

Other famous rocky places were made by people.

At Salisbury, in England, there is a circle of tall rocks, or stones, called Stonehenge.

Ancient people created Stonehenge about 5,000 years ago.

The largest stone at Stonehenge weighs as much as nine elephants!

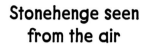
Stonehenge seen from the air

No one knows why Stonehenge was built. Some scientists think it might have been a **temple** that people visited to worship the sun.

Some of the huge rocks were brought to Stonehenge from a place 150 miles (241 km) away. The ancient builders of the stone circle had no trucks or cranes. How do you think they moved the giant stones?

(See page 24 for the answer.)

A Rock City

In the country of Jordan, there is an amazing city called Petra.

Ancient people carved the city out of sandstone rock more than 2,000 years ago.

They carved homes, beautiful rock temples, and **tombs** for burying the dead.

About 20,000 people lived in this famous rock city.

Petra was hidden between mountains. To get into the city, people had to travel along a narrow split in the rocks called the Siq (seek). The Siq is about one mile (1.6 km) long.

the Siq

a temple in Petra

17

Mount Rushmore

Mount Rushmore in South Dakota is famous because it is home to a giant **sculpture**.

The sculpture, which is carved into the mountain's granite, shows the faces of four U.S. presidents.

To make each face, workers first removed large chunks of rock using explosives.

Then they used drills, chisels, and hammers to carve more details.

The workers hung from ropes on the mountainside, hundreds of feet above the ground.

A sculptor named Gutzon Borglum created the Mount Rushmore faces. He began work in 1927. It took Borglum and 400 workers 14 years to complete the sculpture.

President Thomas Jefferson
Each face is about 60 feet (18 m) high.

President Theodore Roosevelt
The presidents' noses are 20 feet (6 m) tall.

President George Washington
Washington's face was carved first.

President Abraham Lincoln
The pupils in the presidents' eyes seem to twinkle. This is because they are made of pieces of granite that are placed to catch the sun's rays.

Famous Rocks Map

This map shows where in the world each of the famous rocky places can be found.

Turnip Rock Island
Lake Huron, Michigan,
United States

Half Dome
California,
United States

Hoodoos at Bryce Canyon
Utah,
United States

The Grand Canyon
Arizona,
United States

Mount Rushmore
South Dakota,
United States

NORTH AMERICA

SOUTH AMERICA

Atlantic Ocean

Pacific Ocean

Stonehenge
Salisbury,
England

The Immortal Bridge
Mount Tai,
China

Mount Everest
Himalaya mountain range,
Border of Nepal and Tibet

Uluru
Northern Territory,
Australia

Petra
Jordan,
Middle East

Arctic Ocean

EUROPE

ASIA

AFRICA

Indian
Ocean

Pacific
Ocean

AUSTRALIA

Southern Ocean

ANTARCTICA

Science Lab

Make a Canyon

The Grand Canyon formed when a river cut a channel through rock.

You can make your own canyon using sand and water.

It's best to do this activity outdoors because it can be messy!

You will need:

- Scooper
- Plastic tray or large baking dish that's about three inches (7.6 cm) deep
- Sand
- Pebbles
- Block
- Watering can or large jug of water

1. Use the scooper to fill the tray to the top with sand. Pack the sand in tight. You can add some pebbles, too.

2. Place a block under one end of the tray so it makes a slope.

3. Slowly pour some water onto the sand at the top of the slope. Then watch what happens.

What do you see happening in the sand?

How is this like what happened at the Grand Canyon?

What do you think you could do to make your canyon deeper?

(See page 24 for the answers.)

Science Words

Aborigine (*ab*-uh-RIJ-uh-nee) a native person of Australia

ancestors (AN-sess-turz) family members who lived a long time ago

canyons (KAN-yuhnz) steep-walled valleys carved out by rivers

sculpture (SKUHLP-chur) a statue or other object made by carving rock

temple (TEM-puhl) a religious building where people go to pray

tombs (TOOMZ) buildings or graves in which dead bodies are buried

Index

Read More

Granger, Ronald. *Exploring Earth's Surface (Exploring Earth and Space).* New York: Rosen (2013).

Jango-Cohen, Judith. *Mount Rushmore (Pull Ahead Books).* Minneapolis, MN: Lerner (2004).

Lindeen, Mary. *History Rocks! (Wonder Readers).* North Mankato, MN: Capstone (2013).

Learn More Online

To learn more about famous rocks, visit
www.bearportpublishing.com/Rock-ology

About the Author

Ellen Lawrence lives in the United Kingdom. Her favorite books to write are those about nature and animals. In fact, the first book Ellen bought for herself, when she was six years old, was the story of a gorilla named Patty Cake that was born in New York's Central Park Zoo.

Answers

Page 15: No one knows for sure how the builders of Stonehenge moved the huge rocks, but scientists have some ideas. The stones may have been put on large wooden sleds that were pulled along the ground by many people or strong animals. Tree trunks may have been placed under the sleds to act as rollers.

Page 22: The water carves a channel through the sand. This is exactly how the Colorado River carved a channel, or canyon, in rock to form the Grand Canyon. To make your sand canyon deeper, try tilting the tray so that the water flows with more speed and force.